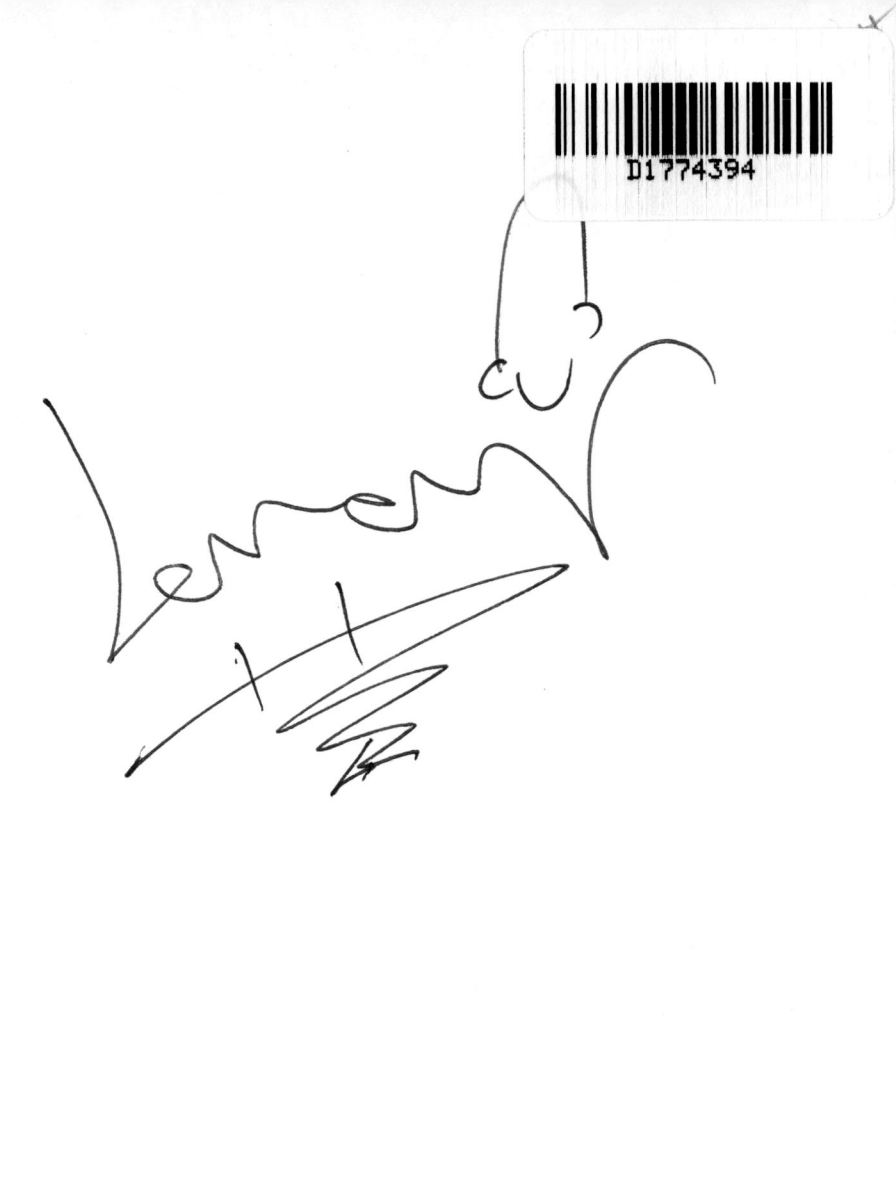

STRAIGHTRAZOR

POEMS
LEMON ANDERSEN

The poem *Noose York* originally appeared in *The Nation*.

Copyright © 2014 Lemon Andersen.

STRAIGHTRAZOR is published by
County of Kings Publishing
c/o 190 Marcy Avenue, #17F
Brooklyn, New York 11211
countyofkingspublishing@gmail.com

All rights reserved. Printed in the United States. No part of this book may be used or reproduced in any manner whatsoever without written permission except in the case of brief quotations embodied in critical articles or reviews. For information please contact the publisher.

Jacket Art: Anthony "AVone" Vasquez
    find him on instagram.com/destroyrebuildny

Book Design: David Vargas
    dvargas77@gmail.com
    http://www.dvargas.viewbook.com/album/dvargas-portfolio#1

Editorial and Production: Paola Soto
    find her on facebook.com/dominicanpie

Photo Credit: Matthew Dean
    find him at www.matthewdeanphotography.com

ISBN 978-0-9761401-39
First Edition: November 2013

STRAIGHTRAZOR

POEMS
LEMON ANDERSEN

For Lisa Andersen

"*I watched a snail crawl along the edge of a straight razor. That's my dream; that's my nightmare. Crawling. Slithering, along the edge of a straight razor . . . and surviving.*"

—Colonel Walter E. Kurtz in *Apocalypse Now*

TABLE OF CONTENTS

Dear Walt Whitman	1
ANAT O' ME	2
HAPPY BIRTHDAY NEPHEW	4
A HARLEM HELLFIGHTER	5
THESE ARE THE BREAKS	9
EDGAR'S BIRD	10
PUNTO	13
"Remember The Time"	14
MMM NEVER!	16
MILLIE'S BOY	17
After nine months	18
A VIETNAM VETERAN	19
DOÑA	21
Born in the river of a hot spoon	22
RATCHET	23
Dear Artist	23
Last night, I snuck into	24
Lemon	25
Nerves	26
NURSERY RHYME	28
FOR TOM	29
YOU THINK	30
POETZ	31
WIRE HANGERS	33
SIGH	34
WRITERS	35
THE FUTURE	36
OYE!	38
YA DIG?	39
DEAR DETROIT	39
WISH ME LUCK	40
I guess	41
The day	42
SOMETIMES	44
NO SLEEP TIL	45
THURSDAYS	46
Dear Nelson Mandela	47
NOOSE YORK	48
L.A.	53
—Black Hooded Sweater	53
RIKERS ISLAND, SMILE	54
ANIMAL KINGDOM	55
WOLF	56
ADULT POEM	58
THUMBS	59
Blessed is a man who has	60
MARILYN	61
PASSPORTLIFE	63
POPS	64
TO THE SINGLE MOTHER AND HER STRUGGLES	65
I SEE YOU BABY, KEEP BANGIN'	66
MY LIPS, GOD'S EARS	67
Lady	68
What is the true story	69
LAWD, LAWD, LAWD	70
LETTERS FROM MY WHITE FATHER	71
PLANK/SPECK	71
C.A.S.E.S	72
DEAR LORD	73
It was winters	74
I tell kids all the time	75
CAN CROONING	76

Dear Walt Whitman . . .

I hear America singing too,
songs of Milwaukee teachers stepping out of their classroom
to two-step with Tameka Jones from the Bronx
the sharecroppers greatest of great grandsons
twirling his wife around the oval office, Dominican perm and all
the mason no longer whistles Dixie in public,
it might not be of the laborers song you once
captured so vividly in verse
many moons have passed
work has changed since then.

Songs have changed . . .

The boatman now sings of cartel and extortion
while the deckhand prays below assault rifle in tow
the shoemaker sings a foreign tune at his bench
as he thinks about his sister adopted by the song of the law.

The woodcutter no longer sings,
he now tap dances his fingers across the keys
yelling at Wall Street in one hundred and forty characters,
with his vintage record player in the back
wailing a Rasta man singing of a rebel song.

The mother is still delicious, still singing, still sewing
still washing but that song is not sung like it use to.
Only a few and far sing.
The hard work song to keep up nowadays for a mother
keeps the kitchen dry, the wash delivered,
denim holes forced into a trend.

Yet like our past we always sing for the nights
and our new songs cost us
years off our lives,
time away from our children
but they will one day understand
that soon they too will also be singing America.

ANAT O' ME

Deep down
there is an old man river
blue denim flow
Martha's Vineyard stepchild
rusty picket fence glow
desert sand
to a black beach bringer
ghetto Shakespearean clown
Little Shop of Horrors fanatic
daydreaming of white girls
from skid row
with black eyes singing downtown
Nuyorican exile
frozen Japan kicks
stacked next to a collection
of homies locked up
posing for Polaroid flicks
suffering from visions of grandeur
sucking the success out of pain
staring at dirty napkins
seeing the art in a coffee stain
cradle to the grave
distant coolness
red wine M.O.
7:30 rudeness
south side outlaw
flying cut sleeves
80 blocks from Tiffany's
on heavy rotated
YouTube bleeds
blood
flooded with anti-social justice
sniffing gunpowder
out of the barrel
of a propaganda musket
immediate descendant of the cool
Veitnam draft

Boriqua mixed
with Lower East Side heroine
resulted in the aftermath
I'm from the house
that Stepin Fetchit
burnt down
lyricist lounge
poet laureate
of the old hip hop underground
son of the drama
child of the Bard
an English soldier at Agincourt
either
die or go hard
kill or be martyrd
iambic pentameter on the regular
so the gift goes farther
an Aristotle thug
dealing with the real
Plato is the enemy of the soul
like a Def Jam deal.

HAPPY BIRTHDAY NEPHEW

Now that you are eighteen
I need to tell you to stay away
from that part of a woman
that tastes like a nine-volt battery.

A HARLEM HELLFIGHTER

for the young ballers

My young mother always told me
keep your hashtags humble
always to keep your grass green
always remain confident
that you were meant
to play amongst the stars
in the field of your dreams.

You see now my daddy
this man was a hustler
who had a charm they say
would shine brighter than the sun
my mother's love for him
was the twenty-four karat necklace
that my daddy's charm
would hang from
both birth me in a time
where the beautiful struggle
finally came into its own
it was known as
the golden era
in that era
they called my dad
"Coogi High"
after the reputation of his product
and his favorite sweaters
but before it got better
that fairy tale surely got worse
the night he left my mother
to see another woman
who set him up with her brothers
I was only six
when he found his new home
only six
watching a six foot pine box
lowered
six feet in the dirt
and although I lived next to the cemetery
that was just a place
I kept at a clear

didn't need a tombstone to remember him
when I keep him right here
his name "Coogi" in calligraphy
on my arms
his initials on my face
right above these tatted tears
and for years after they took
my mother's partner away
she escaped to the drugs
my father smuggled and sold
to numb out the cold burden
of her loneliness
so grandmomma raised me down south only
till my moms got sober . . .

Grandmomma ruled the house
like a porch lady preaching
teaching me
"boy, you are going to have to take revenge
on your daddy's murderers
with prayer and a killer crossover
now in the morning
we are going to see Junior's cousin
who coaches kids out here
so he can put you on a team
you just not going
to be living in my house
when out there
is a world of possibilities
with a field of dreams
I see ya growing up too fast
running wild
now, this ain't the city no more boy,
ya hear me
and I ain't your momma or your daddy
but I'm going to raise you like my child,
you dig."
So I dug knee deep in my studies
waist high up in my sports
physics

soccer field summers
football winters
animal science
but nothing fueled my heart
like the debate team
and that basketball court
first year them big boys
with them funky country long legs
sharp elbows
were running circles
around these Rucker Park skills
learn the hard way
deep in the sticks
having a raw talent
doesn't mean you can be coached
or that you can run drills
second year I learned to guard the perimeter
and my x's and o's after that
never remained the same
then the third year came
and in my game
I worked harder
to put points on the board
polishing pivot blind passes
get more ops for my teammates to score
anted-up my D
found more ways to spread the floor
"I was bangin' on 'em."

Then grandmomma
started gettin' pains in her chest
and my game after that never recovered
from watching my nana fight
a winless battle of cancer in her breast
no clutch shot could save her
so I retired the handles forever
put the ball in the ground
between her and daddy
then laid her soul to rest . . .

Still I will attest
we had a promise
a bond
that I would finish school
cause grandmomma
didn't raise her son,
Coogi's son, to be no fool
so I excelled in science and mathematics,
went to college to study sports fitness,
had a major in critical analysis
a minor in sports business,
I graduated with honors
but being at the top of my class
wasn't greater than what it seems
like the glory
of walking down the aisle
with my mother
clean and sober
in the field of my dreams.

THESE ARE THE BREAKS

Back home in central Bushwick
the old ladies gossip next door
in mountain island machete
and Pentecostal slang
about the black men
their daughters
are sleeping with . . .

I think they are jealous.

Before the word came flying into their
Avon travel sized hands
before they quoted scripture
in Elizabethan Spanish jive
they were screaming,
                          "aye Dios, sigue papi, sigue"
in the back of campos
wiping banana leaves back to front
creating town wars between jibaros
and sleeping with their cousin's cousin . . .

We were all young once
with our legs directing airplanes in the sky.

EDGAR'S BIRD

For when anger
turns to hate . . .

Hate turns
to scuffle
scuffle into brawls
brawls,
battles,
battles into wars
it is because of the raven.

This salted mix of quail and crow
who descends upon our humble abodes
dropping off its parcel
of daunting
padded room dreams,
their haunting.

Bring him here alive
pluckless
let us gather around in a corral
and watch the screws
untighten from its claws,
ungripping the minds
minds freed of knotholes.

Bring me the crown of the raven
so that we can boil it in kerosene,
take away its pride
painful scars,
incinerate its love
suffering burns,
see its ebony blue stare
turn pale in the black night.

Allow it to never circle around
and cipher the gods of madness.

Nightmares are to be awakened
by the blaring star.

Nightmares
no matter how gothic in architecture
exist in a temporary façade,
and yet the raven
deep bile of feathers
born of the melancholy seed
pulls the blinds of the morning sun
and keeps the new day
from turning the frown
upside down.

This bird,
fowl of Hippocrates
turning over graves with its gawking,
perched upon the halo
of a weathered saint,
pecking away at the stoned path
to the heavens,
waiting for the cue of the Reverend
to give the last rites,
crucifying the wind,
waiting for the exodus,
for the families
soaked in sorrow to say farewell,
so it can hover in
finding folly
in the pastel shaded
grey petals of our kin,
scattering the bouquets to and fro.

This symbol of a mad man's smile
reminds the sinner
to pillage the land and leave no fruit
work the children into a dry bosom
motherless labor
in the name of its maker,
the great king apathy.
So go forth with sword and shield,
forth with gun and bow,
seek its keys out of your solitude.
For the loss of a loved one
shall finally have its rest,

its rhythm finally beating
to the tune of time healing,
once the talented ether in the sky
has come home to roost.

Bring me the crown of the raven
or we shall find ourselves
falling off the smokeless chimneys,
head first
hitting the ground
with a thirst
for the murderous
rivers of blood
cold hearted
murderous rivers of blood
and find peace,
nevermore.

PUNTO

I don't need a last name like
Hernandez or Diaz
Ruiz or Calderon
to feel Latino
when I have abuela's Spanish bible
highlighted in pink stains
and bright yellow underlines
marking out the passages
and Psalms
she left behind for the gringo.

                      This all the bloodline I need.

"Remember The Time"

He wore highwaters
fitted fedoras
Gary Indiana chops
black moccasins
white socks
from the ghetto to the block
happy birthday King of Pop
get enough, we won't stop
calling you king, like it or not
giving you Brooklyn love
shine like the rhinestones in your glove.

Today, we name a new Fort Greene
Myrtle Ave. is now Billie Jean Way
say, say
get pleather jackets at Dr. Jays
Twelve inch vinyl *Off the Wall*
bought it cheap Albee Square Mall

Hee-hee-hee
Haw-haw-haw
Heeee

Coney Island Neverland
Red Hook mirror man
south side Williamsburg
"Dirty Diana," ghetto bird
Bedstuy afro
Jackson 5 baby bro'
frontin' future, future frontin'
Fulton "Wanna Be Startin' Somethin'"
East New York Polo boosters
mama say, ma ma coo sa
Nostrand Ave. get that paper
it's in your blood, your "Human Nature"
Brooklyn head to the heels
this is the way you make me feel
Flatbush wah yah say
lick a shot for MJ . . .
He was his mother's son

his father's child
claimed us his party people
moon walked the world to our style
often duplicated,
never repeated
first to do gangster music videos
have you seen "Beat It" . . .

I remember when the killing rate
went down with the crime
cause the whole hood stood home
waiting to see Michael and Eddie Murphy
do "Remember The Time"
we love the speck in his eyes
we loved the plank in his struggles
we loved the way he would show up
to a black-tie event, glittered out
"Rockin' Robin," his monkey Bubbles
Little Baby Boy Blue in heaven
go find your spot in the park
swing, slide, seesaw
you were our shot in the dark
you gave us a better nightlife
fifty-one years of victory . . .

Now enjoy yourself, enjoy yourself
"Enjoy Yourself," for me.

People want you to be "their" version of "your" story.

MMM NEVER!

MILLIE'S BOY

While in a Special Ed. class
A teacher once told my mother,
my sense of learning was too slow
that I was trailing behind
in my academics drastically.

Too bad those textbooks didn't teach
those other students
what my mother taught me that day . . .

"Don't listen to that bitch!"

There was not a damn thing special
about being in special ed,
being labeled emotionally disturbed.

Our tests were ink shit stains on index cards
and visits from children services.

We were separated
from the normal kids in the floors below us.

They had teachers with real last names
like Mr. Smith and Principal Epstein,
instead we called our teachers Mike and John
like that was going to help
        "man, I don't know you like that, sun."

Sometimes we got a chance
to take a mainstream class in the I.S. building
and step out of the old fort of the annex.

The students there seemed to be so clean
so well raised,
into math clubs and had a real gym
that wasn't used as a lunch room or detention hall.

When I went to prison years later
I noticed how the institutional cream colored walls
were the same as the annex,
I guess I should've gotten the hint.

After nine months . . .

Would you still love her,
when she no longer has that look,
those Sin City hips you stalked her for,
when the child puts tiger stripes
around the piercings of her belly,
would you leave her by herself
there in her dark corners
to deal with her transformations,
or is the man going to loosen his tie
take off his gold bottoms,
walk over to his young matriarch
crown her with besos
on the back of her shoulders
she is looking out
into a new view of an old window,
just tell her in rose colored words and Sunday faith,

"we are going to be alright, baby."

A VIETNAM VETERAN

Gifted with poetry and story
drafted away to war
left me a letter before he passed on from AIDS
to see his Lord
how ashamed he was to let his only son down
the war left him Cambodian scars
and tablespoon epilepsy
yet nothing compared to the weight
of his heart when his child
walked him through the doors at Calvary.

I miss this man dearly
the Knicks games I owed him
next to Spike Lee courtside
my wonderful white boy of a pops
wasn't around long enough
to make me fall in love with the Mets
but I root for them
just for him
behind closed doors.

Always wanted to ask
please, tell me why
out of all women
he saw fire in my mother
when she would've beat him
with his own rib
for staring at another lady
crossing the Bruckner.

There are these rearview mirror envies
I have sometimes,
wishing for his blue eyes
how the cameras would wrap around
the soul of them marbles deep in dialogue
but I have to settle for his paper heart
Millie's iron blood
the love,
I have for counting words

in the lyrics of our songs
come from a Red Hook private
who sits in the empty seat
at the theatre every now and then
to watch his son
fight for the 'e' in Andersen.

DOÑA

I live to make old Spanish women,
laugh like this,

        "Cua, cua, cua, cua, cua . . .

                            Sangano!"

Born in the river of a hot spoon

Children of the methadone generation,
detox your stories
for the sake of your smile
kick for your parents' contradictions
somehow they just wanted to love
by their own rules.

The addictions you were born with
can be the highs on life
you can't live without, dig.

To be able to play out their dreams
in travels around the world,
name chapters of your short stories
after their favorite pastimes.

Boys and girls
of the liquid handcuff crew
find liberty in your folks, take notes
on all the teeth that rotted away,
the veins that no longer
look dressed to impress . . .

The Planet of the Apes
is the size of the monkeys
they had on their back
when the thought passed of
finally getting clean.

Generation,
"Why, you had to leave me,
where were you when I needed a momma to fight for."
"No, you are not coming around the bend now that I made it."
"You are dead to me, pops . . ."

If it took their loss for you
to gain the world
then that one stop
at the church on their way to the clinic,
that one bent knee and hard prayer
of, "Lord please for the sake of my children"
got answered.

RATCHET

I love watching Latino relationships
break up
in public . . .

    "It's not you, it's me. Tina."

    "No, fuck . . . you nigga."

Dear Artist . . .

If you want to feel like
you are the only one.

You are in the wrong
business, sun.

It takes a village.

Last night, I snuck into

the old abandoned Kings Theatre
looking for an aisle seat,
within its scattered rows of felt and muse
stood up on seat A, aisle 12
high on top of its broken armrest
and yelled out to the vaudeville ghosts
hidden behind the ravaged interior
walnut paneling and opulent opulence
beaten.

Yelled out to the haunting,
"I know you are there players,
I see you handlers
of lights and sound,
immigrant ushers
still posted by the entry,
even you too popcorn lady
with all that curvature,
you keep battin' your eyes at me
cause it's working.
Darling get your tassels ready,
as well as all you gallant men from Local 1
hiding behind the curtains stage left
I see you without these eyes.

You all better get your
shoes decked to the nine
cause come this time next year
the lights will shine bright
on the wonder of Flatbush Avenue.

This palace of fine arts will soon be richer
than a tycoon with all its majesty
you hear me."

Lemon . . .

No matter how great you are
with the words,
no matter how much you
can jump around wit' it.

The story has to come
from
the deepest part of you
like right there deep,
from the bottom of your balls.
—Suzan Lori Parks '09

. . . Nerves

Anxiety sucks . . .
Megatron tea bags
cause it usually comes
from the bad echoes of a driven heart,
from a lawless ambition
from the suffering of strong will,
life becomes scarred
with walk the plank nerves
even while you sleep
fighting a hereditary disorder
you have to order
to the corner of the room
like a bastard son,
shame most of us have it
but rather drop a pill
than drop a dime,
the chemical vodka and milk
mix in your brain
having a mind of their own
beating your heart like a speed bag sparring
in the ring of "Why me?"

With short inhales of Hail Mary's
large betwixt lungs
and all you're doing
is sitting down trying to enjoy the sun,
caffeine becomes the enemy
of whatever Promised Land,
worry anchors you down to the moat
and its dark lake gives
your steel pride a copper colored phobia,
paper bags work better than hugs,
Xanax, no water please,
Prozac takes too long to kick in,
being in the emergency room
is better for the lighting under your skin,
the therapist who shows up too late
just tells you something
you already googled

and gmailed to your journal
but be reminded
in the tortoise and hare race
of your thoughts
that you are not the only,
the lonely,
no matter how much even crowds of two
shorten your breath
no matter how much you miss population
you have to learn to love
your solitary confinement
even if it palpitates your ticker
like Mexican jumping beans,
pulls the cool out of you,
strip searches you
of your genuine smile
makes your uglies feel public
breaks down your cojones
and makes them feel like lentil,
be reminded that you are normal,
your idols suffer
from the same defects
it is those stubborn rattlesnakes
that make their art divine
those same cryptic complexes
that make up a performance
and not an act
those same tragedies behind
the crescent comedies
that make it magic.

Even the gifted are cursed,
the poor in spirit
wealthy with rich flaws
being good comes with a price
being great comes with a bounty,
you have what they call
a champion sound
being a one hit wonder
is not good for your soundtrack
so you panic with your cold snares
and limited drum samples
always living like their is a beat missing called the big easy.

NURSERY RHYME

The hardest part about my writing
is keeping a pamper on a two year old . . .

Every morning
while the plot thickens,

"hey, did you just pee on the floor?
You are a princess and princesses don't pee on the floor!"

Staring at me with those lake water colored eyes,
sucking on a baby bottle filled with cereal neché,
she pulls it out, burps the smell of puppy water into the sky
to tell me in her baby slang . . .

"I not a princess, I . . .
I'm a monster."

FOR TOM

A great artist and friend once asked me,
"How do you do it? How do you work
and play in so many different worlds.
At one moment you are in the streets
with your friends blowing life into a dice game,
the next second you are
in a regional theatre talking Chekov and Wilson."

    "I don't know the difference
    between how the bright lights
    shine on the decks of that stage
    or how the street lamp glows
    on the corner store hustler . . .

    Either way,
    once the lights go up

    it's show time."

YOU THINK...

you are beautiful,
till you get to Hollywood and you
find out everyone is beautiful.

You think you are talented,
till you get to New York and find
out everyone is talented.

You finally look in the mirror
and find out everyone is
not you.

Bank on that.

POETZ

I love everything about
the world of poets,
the flaws
of new poets
trying to find their flow,
the unlicensed critics
smashing the pop culture poets,
the nerd bad two step poets
breaking character in their focus,
priceless,
the internationally known
locally rejected poets
who teach us about the world
in 4D
when books put too much hurt
on the eyes,
the liberals still holding on to Mumia
it's called frontline loyalty,
take notes.

The young poets
with their one sided Bay Area style
that only they understand
but their a million deep so get over it,
the poets using spoken word
to land a record deal,
somebody is listening to them!
The erotic poets who go down
on a one night stand,
I live vicariously through you,
the poets with a hundred gods
and the ones who believe you can
find God in a "Bazooka Joe" comic strip . . .

The gay poets and their straight parents
who have no choice
but to love them or "eat shit"!
The poets who have 9 to 5 jobs
who don't want to do magic tricks
and back flips they just got somethin' to say, say it baby . . .

The captain save a nigga poets
don't touch their mentorship money
cause that pays for the chap books and hobo traveling,
the baby-mother poets
and their shot at finally
being loved randomly,
the slam poets who go
for each other's caskets at finals
but are each other's pallbearers . . .

When it's all said and done,
when the pen is finally finished
with the page and the last poet is called on stage . . .

We all we got!

WIRE HANGERS

While the neighbors
were beating the fast life
out of their kids next door
and the addicts were begging
Milagros for credit
I learned to tune it all out
with
Masterpiece Theatre and *NOVA*.

SIGH

One day I told my lady in bed
with a heavy heart,
I wanted to get a day job
that I missed being normal,
the spring to my step as a
talent bears a horrible winter
so horrible sometimes it hurts my knees
and she began to cry,
I asked "why are you so upset?"

She told me that if I make that move,
I would die an early death
that my epitaph would only read,
what could've been . . .

I tell her,
        You know how much I hate the fear
        of deep rabbit ears
        Langston's pockets,
        to swing Haymakers at the only painting
        Van Gogh
        sold while he was alive
        who wants
        to only be known as a genius, huh?
        and yes I worry about that fate
        how my children will be burdened
        by the rowing boats of people singing,
        "your father changed my life"
        how the pearls will roll in their eyes
        and they will envy
        the banker's daughter.

WRITERS

If you see me walking
down the street talking
to myself,
it's not cause I'm crazy,
I'm trying to find
the old man by the river.

THE FUTURE

Let it top the Billboard charts
four score
years a thousand fold
till everyone realizes
the truth will go pop,
the honest and upright
will bang in the club,
lying will only list you
with the sucker MCs
Grammys will be overrated
and oxymoronic
ghost writing will win the Pulitzer
slang will evoke change,
break beats will become elevator music
car navigation
will use top to bottom graff walls
to get you through traffic
grandmothers will still
be making music with their mouth Biz,
thugs will finally come out
and tell the world
that they are the real
hip hop masons
wearing baggy jeans
under your ass
will come back permanently
tattoos will be earned
dreads will be licensed
only to the nappy
the party people will strike
against DJs using MP3s
studios will be strapped
with lie detectors
rappers will replace video hoes
with their wives and kids
MC Lyte will be our new Oprah
the Oscar will go to Lupe Fiasco
for playing Rakim

we will wake up every morning
and pray south to the Bronx
we will have a hip hop high school
for the ignorant but blissful
where they will teach
master classes on beat boxing
field trips to old train yards
horticulture classes
on who can grow the best kush,
Big L's rhyme books
will be the basis for all English majors
we will live in a world ruled
by the iron fist of the 8-0-8,
"It Was A Good Day" by Ice Cube
will be illustrated into a children's book,
they will paint the Brooklyn Bridge
red, black, and green
to commemorate Spike Lee,
they will finally be
some honor amongst us
see *America's Most Wanted*
will run an hour special
on who killed Jam Master Jay
Hollywood will move to Atlanta
for balance
L.A. will celebrate their independence
from the entertainment industry
we will respect
our gold chains
our diamonds
and replace them
with Steve Biko name plate quotes
democracy will fall into the hands
of an OG'd out government
where Dead Prez will be in charge
of the People's Army of the United States,
Latifah will be the first lady
"Ladies First"
and what do you know
Eric B. will be President.

OYE!

All these young actors of color
need better writers,
you got
their soul all wrong . . .

Where's the onion and who is
the peeler?

YA DIG?

Transition is straight kicking my ass right now, thank God for the Mike Tyson theory . . .

"Whenever they are beating you bite their ear off."

DEAR DETROIT . . .

Take your New Yorkers back.
They need you.

WISH ME LUCK

Found a new cafe in Bushwick to work out of
feels like an old biker's club with gang disciplines
Puerto Ricans and black lovers quarrel
the smell of melted heroine spoons
still sugarcane sweet in the air.

I asked the lady behind the counter,

                "what was this place before you moved in?"

She pointed to the old tin carburetor sign above
shaped like a fraternity paddle
I knew I was right
yup, this is the place for me and
the orphans
to find a new home before the rapture comes
and someone walks in speaking French
that is the sign
it is time to move the work again
pit stop deep into the solitude
of Brownsville.

I guess . . .

Growing up I always thought impossible was short for
"I am possible"
so when people told me, "no, that's impossible"
I took it as faith.

The day . . .

Rosie Perez
showed her disco tight
lightning hips
and mama Africaña lips
in the opening credits
of *Do The Right Thing*
I knew the truth that
the Nuyorican soul
would be immortalized in pictures.

I sat there in a Bensonhurst dollar
movie matinee
next to Vinnie and Jackie Boy
stuck at seeing someone
who looked like my sister
front and center
Public Enemy rattling
Bedford-Stuy backdropped
crunch pedal
brownstone horn blaring
Professor X cutting,
"what you got to say?"
At the ones
mixing "yeahs" at the twos . . .

Rosie was going in for us
dancing like she own that vinyl first
glowing thrilla in manilla
Everlast shorts
vanilla dipped in ebony
our ghetto child
before you heard her voice squeak
"Mookie" you knew
she was going to be
a poster on your wall
next to that bonita bandera y que

if it wasn't for that day
I would have never known
our sister could look so good
standing up to a Black man
talking about,
"what you gonna do Mookie?"
baby in hand like I was there
sleeping on the couch
in that scene
never before did you see
the love filmed
between Blacks and Boriquas
till the Mayor of Brooklyn
wrote it in short hand
and set it off
let it jump on the big screen
that we Black like that.

In Brooklyn, baby.
Puerto Ricans and Black love
go way back like
Dominicans and the middle passage
Cubans and Nile River congeros
the Colons y los Jacksons
Tina and Mookie
and the hottest day that summer.

SOMETIMES...

I stand on the corner of
Broadway and Marcy
just to hear the drums
clack clackin'
under the elevated train.

Can't learn that beat at the Bard.

NO SLEEP TIL. . .

As a child
when I saw Dorothy close her eyes
and whisper loudly,
"there is no place like home"
I didn't understand that word

                                        "Home."

Till I saw *The Warriors*
make it back to Coney Island
then I knew
what she was talkin' about.

THURSDAYS

Growing up my homies would say to me after a rooftop cypher,

    "yo, sun . . . where you going?"

"Headed to see Shakespeare in the Park."

    "What-the-fuck-is-that, yo?"

"Man, just bunch of fools rapping about their world, that's all."

    "Cool, yo be careful."

Dear Nelson Mandela...

As an 80s baby from New York,
I remember the day you were liberated
from a South African prison
and made your way to the states,
you took a pit-stop in Bedstuy during a time
when this neighborhood
was one of the most dangerous places in the world
but that was a sign
that your heart has always been on the front line,
as you make your transition to meet your maker
I just want to put it out there
that we recognize your presence and we owe you
a statue at Boys and Girls High School
dipped in bronze and mad love
for showing up for us when no one
would dare step foot on Fulton Street.

Madiba...

NOOSE YORK

Waiting for a Crown Victoria
on the corner of Central and Putnam
in the Bushwick section of Old Medina.
Waiting here on the corner
for a Crown Victoria which finally shows up
after running past a traffic light
without the thought of a fast child
crossing the street
chasing her mother's milk
grocery list in hand.

Pulling up to a hard stop
heavy footed brake
the car doors unlock in a dominos spill.
The driver jumps out
points his finger and barks.
"What are you doing here,
got any drugs on you buddy?"

This is not the cab
I was waiting for,
not the Spanglish taxi-man
who always tells me on my way to JFK
I could get more bang
for my dollar Americano
if I spend my money in D.R.

"Static, static."

His partner
who jumps out of the passenger side
with a walkie-talkie chirping
is shaped like a radio DJ
too many crack of dawn diners in his blood.
He grips his pistol and also barks.
"Hey big guy, where were you coming from?"

The kids up the block
take their eyes off the moon
and I am center stage
under that same moon luminous

against the storefront dry cleaner,
shoved toward the cold glass
by the hype man behind the badge
face pressed tough against the cold glass,
needle and thread neon sign rata-tat-tatting.

I stare at the Selena shaped tailor sewing inside.
Wanting to speak, even if I stutter,
I still have to utter the words
to these officers
for those kids who were staring at the moon,
for their older brothers,
their uncles dragging their back aches
back from a prideful hard days labor.

Wanting to speak for them with valor
capture for these blue bloods
the beautiful confidence
snatched everyday on this corner
I pull out the heart to say,
 "yes sir, no . . ."
An empty can crooning,
 "no sir, yes . . ."

The rhythm less words cut off by the rattlesnakes
these nerves cut short by the quotas
because history on this corner has proven
that collars have to be made
by the end of the month
and these backward numbers have nothing
in common with real suspects
real crimes
like outta town gun laws and Walmart shoppers.

I go over the speech in my head.
"What are you going to arrest me for, officers?"
Shit, that's easy.
"Do I look suspicious by the trends I wear
for standing on the corner waiting for a cab?
On the corner of a street you don't own."
Damn, too liberal.
"Sir, why do these men

only get stopped for being black,
for owning their brown skin?"
That is it! That's the stinger.

But just then
the radio DJ checks my chin and my pockets
while his partner
kicks my legs wide and to the side,
and I finally yell out.
"Do you even know who Israel Putnam was?"

Intermission . . .

"Do you know this corner was named after
an American Revolutionary
who killed the last remaining wolf of
Connecticut in a town called Brooklyn?
You wouldn't know that hype man
cause you did not go to school
to research the beat of your streets,
to uphold the law.
That's right this same corner
Where your guns make me feel like
breathing air is a felony waiting to happen.

Is it because of the way we look?
How does this deep hooded sweater
I wear over my head
come with a license for you to kill
when I wear it to block out the frozen world
while the projects are over heated.
Maybe it's my sneakers?
I bought them for running,
But if I run we all know what happens next.
It can't be the color of my skin
when you both look like distant cousins
if you go back far enough aren't we all . . .

Then again maybe not,
cause in my family we were raised
not to point at people
especially at officers
cause they don't point back with their fingers.

You want to stop and frisk someone,
stop and frisk the mayor
cause his pockets
are low and his money is high
and the teachers are as broke as a joke.
You will get more out of his spare change
than what you can get
out of these rabbit ears right now.

You want to arrest somebody
go arrest that new neighbor across the street.
The one right there double-timing it
with the checkers game flannel shirt
that could be mistaken for gang colors on me.

Arrest him
for not helping the doña next door
with her bags of empanada ingredients
up the stairs
cause he is too busy constructing,
plotting a blue print plan
to open up a Vietnamese restaurant
run by Mexicans,
when doña Margo been dodging hollow tips
right here
on the corner of Central and Putnam
right here,
when your precinct wouldn't even drive
down this block thirty years ago.

You want to arrest me,
arrest me for being honest
cause I was lying before.
The words never came out
never blossomed . . . . Never.
Too scared of this new city
pushing me out
too many front page posts
warning me
it will be my word against yours.
The truth is that you know like I know.

That a law like stop and frisk
is built to send
more Puerto Ricans to Orlando
blacks to Camden
and the Dominicans
to Amish country Pennsylvania.
But they will be back when it's over.
Cause they gotta go home.
We all gotta go home.

L.A.

I always thought discrimination was short for:

"Dis-Crime-Is-a-Nation"

In America, where there are stars
there are stripes.
On the wrong side of freedom.
—**Black Hooded Sweater**

RIKERS ISLAND, SMILE

I read
to push the pink slip away
from the factory locker
I read to make those prison bars
near the officers' bubble
look more like an exit gate
with every wake up,
the walls look down on you here
they face-to-face you
like a human resource counselor

I didn't sleep much
when I did,
it's with one eye open
to the murderers and swine stories,
guilty fiction shorts
book ended with state issued soap
carved into a black fist
by a sculptor with a rape charge
that lacks DNA numbers,
say "bye-bye to the bad guy,"
I read cause I had time
I always complained about not having,
time served in military green scrubs
to match my *Ghostbusters* green mug
that makes for a good ashtray
and a sharp weapon
when melted down to the wax
project walls,
prison walls,
hospital floors,
all have the same color:
institutional cream . . .

I know this cause the used books
the hipsters donated to the church,
ended up on my lap,
fed my malnourished food and liquor education
with fine wine and Elizabethan women
and now the world
is bigger than the block.

ANIMAL KINGDOM

What do you tell a kid
who is going to sit in a breadbox
for the rest of his life . . .

Where the whites in his eyes
are colored with fire engine red . . .

There is no sense in telling him
to slow down . . .

All you can do is pray
for the prey
that will be in his way.

WOLF

Today on the cover of the *New York Post* was a gun
behind that gun was a man,
a young man I knew . . .

The headline read:
"She's A Pistol! Cop Kills Thug,
Saves Her Partner!"

Before the incident the young thug
who they say snarled,
was sitting in a woman's house,
crying to a mother that wasn't his
about a life he wouldn't have wished
on Osama Bin Laden
hiding a second gun in broad daylight
opened his broken soul
double bloodshot eyes
between low grade haze
rose bud and tears
strolling up his face to a flirt,
he let her know a life without love
should not live,
should not breathe
uncles with sticky fingers for little boys,
should have their hands cut off
and their wrists slit vertically
across from Greenwood cemetery
the ghosts behind the fence
picnicked on their graves
and watched on this tragedy
like an old pastime.

Today on the cover of the *New York Post* was a gun
behind that gun was a man,
a young man,
a young man I knew,
not rich enough to sand down
the edges of his jail tattoos
he owed polishing,

not strong enough to hold himself
in his loneliness,
the hole in his heart was there
before the hot lead showed up
and knee-danced its way through,
the shackles on his life were there
before the cuffs on his arms came,
he laid there like a skeleton key
with the doors Krazy glued shut
on his padded room dreams.

He complained about the pains
in his head
so they stuck needles in his feet
and the conspiracy haunted him . . .

It takes a real man to love a daughter
he did not put into the world,
her visits to Potter's Field
will die with her teenage love,
the front page dismount of his life
will suffer from jaundice
and a lack of iron.

ADULT POEM

As a kid I watched a pop singer and a songwriter
act out porn on a tar beach,
rolling up fags
talking about Paris,
Amsterdam window shopping
and Prince Street art vendors,
smelling like booty whistling Dixies
pantied ankle bracelets,
her makeup raining
on the tin-roof of his face,
Clockwork Orange boneage.

Watching the beads.
tongue each other down in to sweatlines,
sweatlines into slow drips
slow drips into a full moon shower
the floors below are ravaged
with screaming children
reeking of corn syrup
while the birds and the bees look on
with great smiles and hands in their crotch
hurricane tongues and 70s bushes
cause that's what young sex is about
tonight on the tar beach roof
of a project hallway . . .

THUMBS

I know what it was like
to be without a home
in the blizzards
of this soon to be blanketed city,
warm colored Timbs
frozen high up on a subway bench
not enough geese in my down
to bring the temperature up
watching the bright snow
stack against itself
top of a third rail
blowing into my hands to keep
that pen and pad going
always dreaming, always going . . .
and Wu-Tang was for the children.

Blessed is a man who has
        found his work
           and one woman to love . . .

MARILYN

She smelled of Downy and fried chicken.
and I thought vaya . . .

You must be Puerto Rican
but you look Dominican.
Good even better . . .

This red woman of mine
stamped with a Marcy Ave. address
made up of no makeup
no nail polish
just clear diamond
Broadway Strip Mall lip-gloss
and storefront liquor eyes
such a housing project stare
always ready to roll back and to the left
at every,

"hey ma? ay yo, yo ma!"

I noticed there wasn't a lot of conquest in her blood,
her people must have hid in the mountains
when the raids were going down.
She told me she was
into funny looking white boys
so I got lucky.

When I saw her hands
I thought about Bill Withers at Carnegie Hall.
I knew from that spring morning
in the Dutch county of Havemeyer and South 4th
I found the doña that was going to bury me.

The Lady in the Lake.

Back then,
when her friends asked her,
"why him?"
She knew one day forever they will ask,
"does he have a brother?"
When her mother told her,
"los poetas no saben mantener los hijos"
she winks back now with a pair tickets
for every opening night . . .

61

.ed woman
⹁s done more in my life
than the Coffey Park phoenix
who gave birth to me
and Millie would agree.

She has brought to the world children
the stubborn velvet heart of Heaven
who makes me want to kill every boy
that looks like Justin Beiber
a glowing scrunchie Shine
who does cartwheels at the dinner table
and the Gem of our ocean
our baby, of the baby girls
who hides our keys in places
the boogie man wouldn't go
and destroys our alone time.
It's been two years
and we still can't kick her out of the bed.
No matter how painful the labors,
this red woman will give me more
if I so beckoned.

What's not paid back in riches
is flooded back in the wealth
of this rare dream
I live to love every day.

If I can script this lady
risk her life
to save her father
from his only fear of losing work
to the dark days of dialysis.
She walks around with one kidney
so he can smile again.

Folks always ask
how I crossover the live word hustle
into the biggest brightest lights.
Well, ask this lady of mine,
who buries my head in her chest
and tells me I . . . am . . . possible.

PASSPORTLIFE

Sometimes I want to
tell her how much I love her
with trips around the world
mountain top hammock silence . . .

Drinking the grapes of wrath
watching silent movies
in epic citadels
on the cusp of another time zone
eating fruit off the land
both of us batting our eyes
at the farmer's daughter
crashing overnight at a hostel
teaching dominos to the local kids
gossiping with the mayor of a town
that knows no electricity
bathing each other
in the amazon rivers of our wishes
and then I will tell her
when we get back home . . .

You know I love
to love you, ma.

POPS

Today I told my daughter Heaven,
who did not have a great
relationship with her teacher this year,

                      "sometimes your enemies
                      in the streets, become your
                      best friends in jail."

She looked at me
like I was crazy.

                      Never mind.

TO THE SINGLE MOTHER AND HER STRUGGLES

"What to do with my life?"
You ask
everyone seems to have an answer
fortune cookie quotes,
church gospel
"get up off your ass" sounds easy
"today is the day you begin your new journey"
yeah that's simple,
the truth is,
it's not easy
it's very hard,
you have to grow with these pains
these are the tough mornings you have to get up
and remind yourself
this life is going to kick my ass up
and down Front Street
you can't
but you will
cause you love yourself too much
and the eyes shining on you
from the corner of the room
are the faith you need to know exists
when you stop believing in yourself
that child
those children
will watch you fight
to find your position in the sun
in turn
they will turn fighters
themselves
by law
so here is a fortune cookie quote . . .

If you had to hitchhike on the side of a hard road
for your babies to pick you up in a fancy car one day
and take you for the ride of your life,
that hard walk up the stubborn hill
to the freeway of love
was worth it.

I SEE YOU BABY . . .
KEEP BANGIN' . . .

When she doesn't have the words
to speak what's truly deep in her soul
when she is too busy taking
care of her babies
while her friends enjoy the freedoms
of sex,
drugs, and rock-and-roll
when she locks herself away
with a cigarette and tears
to finally find some piece of mind
no one will tell her
that there
is a beautiful struggle
written in between the lines.

MY LIPS, GOD'S EARS

So she learns to love from a distance
sending her new man
text hugs
instead of the naked grips
tender scratches
biting lips . . .

She don't play this time around
he hates her
when she stares too much
into the kettle bells of the past
weighing her down
away from trying to love again
without risk.

The last fuck that cut
that deep
really cut that deep,
he is new and naive
eye candy for the flossing
so her friends
her family
can keep the wool
over their despise for the
memories of a love she still
sits in her closet
kicking herself
for
there is no rehab for the jones
of a soul mate.

Lady . . .

Before I become your man,
first I need to learn how to be a man
or you will get up and leave me
for the door
and that door hurts baby
but when I become a man
you can go ahead and leave me for the door
cause I will be strong enough
to rip the hinges off
and go get my woman back.

What is the true story . . .

Behind the bottle service girl
at the club?
With all that hour glass body
do the heels ever come off
when she clocks out
the hair unpinned, can she
walk anywhere in public
or are the cabs always on speed dial
does she ever look at men the same
after thousands of fingers
have slipped cross the lines.

A stripper in Sin City once told me,
"I love your poetry"
and I never went back
it was the first time I saw
my father's hands,
I left the singles at the bar
and thought about the mirrors
they danced in front of that night
it seemed like every magic trick
was all style and no heart,
big tips were just a round
of empty applause . . .

LAWD, LAWD, LAWD

She preached Christ
with extreme
and great conviction
on the local-n-caboose
heading into old Dutch country
took a moment of silence
to let the auto-tuned conductor say
"ladies and gentlemen
we are being held momentarily,"
before she jumped back in
our faces to release our demons . . .

I wanted to tell her
"sister, I need lust back,
cause I'm on my way
to the strip club
and these women are
hollering for a dollar
and they will smell
your gospel all over me."

LETTERS FROM MY WHITE FATHER

Don't marry
a Puerto Rican woman
if you are not willing to die for her,
cause she will kill you anyway . . .

But better to have loved and lost,
even if it's your own life.

PLANK/SPECK

You left her cause she was crazy . . .
Crazy enough to be with you!

C.A.S.E.S

Such a young hopeful,
if you spent
the same amount of time daily
to open up a word
as you do gutting and splitting
open a vanilla Dutch Master,
with such craft in a decade's time
you will gain a voice
for the critics to boil in oil
and not lose your mind
in the dark patches of your lungs.

DEAR LORD

Don't bless me with luck,
bless me with hard work
so I can keep that luck forever.

—Courtyard Saint

It was winters . . .

like these
in the golden era of the Empire State
where us young hustlers
played the corner Laundromat close for gloves
and no matter how frozen the grind
the baby still needs milk
and them Jordan-sevens are dropping in two weeks . . .
long live the grizzly.

I tell kids all the time

to stay away from four letter words,
especially the word "fear."

CAN CROONING

See that horizon
ghetto children of the world.
That is us, our stories
divided by earth and sky.

Don't ever let them tell you
your struggle ain't a beautiful thang,

no generation changed the game
like our dice for the last twenty-five joints,
never let the devils pardon your slang,
every twang
every Jive talk got a heartbeat
every street corner symphony
got a accent that bleeds
blood like a scholar.

Find your story in places untapped like the opera, the theatre,
debate societies
sci-fi narratives
connect your turf to the sun.

Who will tell you no if all you gotta do is be great . . .

Also By
LEMON ANDERSEN

The Award Winning Book Based on the Critically Acclaimed Staged Memoir

County of Kings
by Lemon Andersen
978-0-9761401-0-8
$14.99/$17.99 Can.

"Mr. Andersen has a distinctive talent that makes words sing in a way that insist you listen." —*New York Times*

"In compelling and well-performed iambics, whose artfulness somehow takes the hurt out the horror, Andersen evokes and enacts the barbarous Brooklyn of his youth."—*New Yorker*

"The language in Andersen's show is so much fun that it's tempting to quote the entire script..."—*Variety*

"In a masterful blend of verse, rap and dialogue, Andersen paints a highly original portrait of his beloved urban wonderland..."–*Associated Press*

Available Now on Amazon